21 DAY DEVOTIONAL

Deborah Hilton

Written and published by Deborah Hilton
Email: deborahannehilton@gmail.com facebook: facebook.com/IsayYES/
Blog: debsblog.space/

Copyright © Deborah Hilton, 2023

All rights reserved. No part of this publication may be reproduced, stored in or introduced into a database and retrieval system or transmitted in any form or any means (electronic, mechanical, photocopying, recording or otherwise) without the prior written permission of the publisher.

Scripture quotations marked (GNT) are taken from the Good News Translation in Today's English Version- Second Edition Copyright © 1992 by American Bible Society. Used by Permission.
Scripture quotations marked (TLB) are taken from The Living Bible copyright © 1971. Used by permission of Tyndale House Publishers, Inc., Carol Stream, Illinois 60188. All rights reserved.
Scripture quotations marked (TPT) are from The Passion Translation®. Copyright © 2017, 2018, 2020 by Passion & Fire Ministries, Inc. Used by permission. All rights reserved. ThePassionTranslation.com.
Scripture quotations marked (NIV) are taken from the Holy Bible, New International Version®, NIV®. Copyright ©1973, 1978, 1984, 2011 by Biblica, Inc.® Used by permission. All rights reserved worldwide.
Scripture quotations marked (NLT) are taken from the Holy Bible, New Living Translation, copyright ©1996, 2004, 2007, 2013, 2015 by Tyndale House Foundation. Used by permission of Tyndale House Publishers, Inc., Carol Stream, Illinois 60188. All rights reserved.
Scripture quotations marked (NASB) are taken from the New American Standard Bible®, Copyright © 1960, 1962, 1963, 1968, 1971, 1972, 1973, 1975, 1977, 1995 by The Lockman Foundation Used by permission.
Scripture quotations marked (MSG) are taken from THE MESSAGE. Copyright © by Eugene H. Peterson 1993, 1994, 1995, 1996, 2000, 2001, 2002. Used by permission of NavPress. All rights reserved. Represented by Tyndale House Publishers, Inc.
Scripture quotations marked (NCV) are taken from the New Century Version®. Copyright © 2005 by Thomas Nelson. Used by permission. All rights reserved.
Scripture quotations marked (ERV) are taken from the Easy To Read Version. Copyright © 2006 by Bible League international
Scripture quotations marked (AMP) are taken from the Amplified® Bible, Copyright © 1954, 1958, 1962, 1964, 1965, 1987 by The Lockman Foundation Used by permission.
Scripture quotations marked (CSB) are taken from The Christian Standard Bible. Copyright © 2017 by Holman Bible Publishers. Used by permission. Christian Standard Bible®, and CSB® are federally registered trademarks of Holman Bible Publishers, all rights reserved.

ISBN: 9780994636249 (paperback); 9780994636256 (ebook)

 A catalogue record for this book is available from the National Library of Australia

Edited by Jo Sutton
Book Design by Lara Taylor
Cover photo and page images by Clem Onojeghuo on Unsplash
Photo of Deborah Hilton by Paul Hilton

Printed and bound in Australia, United States or United Kingdom by IngramSpark, Lightning Source Inc.

About the Author

Let me tell you a little about myself. I've been serving alongside my husband Paul in Asia with Australian Christian Churches International for over 25 years. Over the years, we've grown an organisation which helps communities develop and thrive — body, soul and spirit — and in turn, model the same for others in their community. While still based in Asia, we now coach, mentor and pastor others who also serve God cross-culturally. My passion is to see men and women of all ages rise up and pursue the call of God on their life and become a positive influence in their world. I'm an Author and Speaker and also the Co-Developer of the life skills program Flourish for women.

About the Devotional

I've called this 21-day devotional 'Step Out' because that's what it takes to see the unfolding of your dreams, call, and purpose. This devotional is derived from my book 'Just Say YES'. See an overview of that book below.

It is a known fact that it takes at least 21 days to begin to form a habit — 66 days for it to become behavior. My goal is to see you form a habit or break one, so you can step into your God-given call. During these next 21 days, you'll discover how you can trust God in your own journey with Him. I will challenge you to put what you read into action each day, so you find yourself walking in the will and purposes of God.

About 'Just Say Yes'

'Just Say YES' is written in three parts.

Part 1: My story — This first part tells the early part of my story. The takeaway here is that no matter what your past was like, or what challenges you've faced, you don't have to be defined by your past.

Part 2: The Tassie experience. This section takes you on my 'Bible School of life' journey with God, which took place after obeying His call to move from our hometown to a new unfamiliar place — Tasmania (Tassie). I learnt that answering God's call doesn't mean that everything will go smoothly or look exactly how we expect it to. In this season, I learnt to dig deep wells with God and found Him to be faithful in every area of my life.

Part 3: 200 days of miracles. Here you'll take a 200-day walk with me and God. When God called my family from Australia to Asia, I asked Him to give me something every day until we got on that plane. In those 200 days, I discovered how deep, how wide, how high, how faithful and how much more magnificent He is than I had ever understood before.

Destined for Purpose

If I asked you what your purpose in this life is, would you be able to articulate this for me? Do you believe you have a destined purpose? Maybe you know that you've been put on this earth for a reason, but aren't sure what it is and how to step into it. Whatever the case, God, our creator, tells us very clearly that He has destined us for a purpose and He desires us to fulfill that purpose.

For we are God's handiwork, created in Christ Jesus to do good works, which God prepared in advance for us to do. Ephesians 2:10 (NIV)

Before beginning this 21-day devotional 'Step Out', here are some simple questions to assist you in both knowing how to recognise your calling and communicate it effectively.

- What do you instinctively gravitate to?
- What are you naturally good at?
- What grabs your attention / what are you dreaming about?
- What have friends, family or those in ministry spoken over you about your calling?

Answering these four questions should help you articulate your answer to the following:

- What is your why?
- And why do you want to know and step into your purpose?

Remember, it's your 'why' that's the most important. It's your 'why' that will get you up in the morning, no matter how you feel or what the day in front of you holds.

Take some time to answer these questions before diving into this 21-day devotional. While you're contemplating your responses, I'll answer these questions about myself to assist you with the process.

Deb's Call

What do you instinctively gravitate to?
I've always been fascinated with those who serve God as missionaries.

At the young age of around 13, I began receiving pamphlets in the mail from those serving in Africa. I would find my mind wandering to that unfamiliar place and imagine living there. When I grew up and got married, the church we were attending had a focus on Sri Lanka which saw my interest grow towards that nation. Although I didn't consider myself a missionary at the time, nor did I think it was possible, it was obviously something that continued to grab my attention.

Other areas such as speaking and writing also grabbed my attention, however I didn't give them as much thought, even though I journaled regularly.

What are you naturally good at?
This is an interesting question. Although I wasn't confident, nor believed in myself, I've always been good at marketing. I love to 'sell' what I believe in. Many years ago, I was stifled in my natural gifting by a so-called friend who told me I was bossy. Those words went into my spirit and for a long time I believed that I should be silent — to not have an opinion about anything, nor share my ideas or speak in public. I overcame this negative comment through the encouragement of those who knew me and by choosing to believe what God said about me. I also started focusing on my 'why' — being to serve cross-culturally, and to see others grow and motivate them to be all God has called them to be.

Note: Be on your guard, because the very thing God has designed and wired you for, the enemy will attack.

What grabs your attention / what are you dreaming about?
For many years, my attention was captured by seeing the communities we worked in be empowered and discover the resources they had within them and around them — as individuals, families and whole communities. I often found myself dreaming of what else we could be doing to assist the beautiful people in this Asian nation to realise their own dreams.

I'm now in a new season where God has shifted my attention from being hands on, to pouring out to others what my husband and I have learnt, and sharing the experience we've gained through the ministry we've led for over 25 years.

What have friends, family or those in ministry spoken over you about your calling?
Everything that I've mentioned so far has been spoken over me. 'You're called to the nations.' 'You're called to speak.' 'You're called to write.'

The call to the nations sat well with me (and my family). The call to speak excited me, although I felt completely unqualified. The idea of writing a book was almost laughable to me, as I hardly read books. I had no experience writing, yet I have since written two books, not including this devotional. All of these areas which were stirring in me — some of which were evident and one which was not — God had designed in me long ago. As I opened myself up to these areas and stepped into them, God made a way for each of these areas to become a reality.

What is your why? And why did you want to know and step into your purpose?
What an important question. My 'why' had to be genuine otherwise whatever I put my hand to would only last until the honeymoon period was over. My God purpose caused me to put a stake in the ground and no matter what challenges came my way, I would respond with, 'I may not understand the reason for challenges, twists and turns, as well as the highs and lows, but I know I'm where God wants me, and what He has called me to do.'

Firstly, my purpose.

To serve cross-culturally.
I had no idea what that looked like when I began my journey, and it didn't work out how I imagined in my mind. However, as I stuck with the process it all became clear and God used me (and my family) in a way that was more than I could have possibly asked or imagined, and with greater fruit than I could've ever envisaged.

To speak publicly.
God has opened up many doors of opportunity for me to speak. The first time was terrifying. I was in the bathroom until it was time to step on stage. Since then, I've learnt that my confidence is in God's ability to anoint and speak through me.

To write.
Writing has become a growing passion. I'm constantly thinking about my next blog or my next book. I've co-written a life skill program which is now used worldwide. Who knew! I didn't, until I stepped out with baby steps and saw God bless it, and the Holy Spirit creatively breathe on it.

Now, my why.

Others.
I love seeing others succeed and be all that God has called them to be — to walk in their calling in a healthy way. To thrive and not just survive, so they, in turn can see others in their world do the same. Besides the love and deep passion I have for my family, this is what gets me up in the morning.

Communicating my purpose.
I'm called to minister and serve cross-culturally. To pastor/coach/mentor both local nationals and those who are also called to minister cross-culturally. I've been anointed by God to speak and write for the purpose of seeing others unlocked into their calling.

Now, it's your turn.

You can write down dot points, or write as you would speaking to a friend. Whatever works for you. This will be your launching pad as you begin this 21-day devotional.

....
....
....
....
....
....
....
....
....
....
....
....
....
....
....
....
....
....

Part I
Navigating Your Call

Day 1

DON'T RISK YOUR DESTINY

No amount of difficulty — whether persecution, affliction or any resistance you're experiencing — will stop you from fulfilling God's purpose for your life, if you're fully committed to Him and to following His leading.

Sometimes when we step out, those difficulties and challenges seem to intensify. Does that mean we're going in the wrong direction? Absolutely not. In fact, it's quite possible those very things are indicators we are indeed going in the right direction.

When my husband, Paul and I stepped out in preparation to serve God overseas, we began to experience a lot of opposition. It would've been easy to question what we were doing. Choosing to stay tuned into God's voice in the midst of those difficulties, made room for us to hear Him speak. He said, 'Those giants that you are yet to slay will not stop you from fulfilling your purpose, as long as you stay focused and committed to the journey that I am taking you on. Don't miss my signposts, my everyday confirmations. Keep watch for them so you don't miss one of them.'

There would be nothing worse than missing the signposts God was pointing out to us and finding ourselves going around in circles. This would be a total waste of time and energy! When deciding to stand up and move into the call of God, it's easy to look at the challenges or obstacles that stand in our way and say; 'This is not right'. Or worse still, 'This is too difficult.' We need to keep our eye on the guide — who is God — and listen to His voice. He will point out each landmark, helping us navigate the twists and turns on the journey to the destination He has prepared for us.

What does the Word of God say?

This God is our God forever and ever; He will lead us for all time to come.

Psalm 48:14 (GNT)

I will instruct you (says the Lord) and guide you along the best pathway for your life; I will advise you and watch your progress. Don't be like a senseless horse or mule that has to have a bit in its mouth to keep it in line!

Psalm 32:8-9 (TLB)

Your word is a lamp to guide me and a light for my path.

Psalm 119:105 (GNT)

A man's mind plans his way [as he journeys through life], But the Lord directs his steps and establishes them.

Proverbs 16:9 (AMP)

Questions

Can I suggest, that besides answering the questions I have for you each day, you also journal your own thoughts, and what God speaks to you about through the Holy Spirit?

Even if journaling is not usually your thing, I strongly encourage you to at least write down a few dot points. I cannot emphasise enough how much you'll discover — and how much God will reveal to you — by putting pen to paper, or making notes on your computer.

Ask God to prepare your heart as you 'Step Out', beginning with these 21 days.

Don't rush the process.

It's your life we're talking about here.

Take one step at a time.

When we say YES to God's plans, our eyes must stay fixed on the 'plan maker'.

Q: What's one step you are willing to take today to move towards your God-given purpose?

....

....

....

....

Q: What do you need to do to put that one step into action?

....

....

....

....

Q: Who can you confide in to keep you accountable on your journey?

> That person needs to be an encourager; one who will spur you on to be all you're called to be. That person must be someone who won't judge you but will remind you of why you're doing this.

....

....

....

....

Day 2

THOSE LITTLE DISTRACTIONS

Distractions. The things that divert our attention from the main thing.

When Jesus called people to follow Him in Luke 9:57–62 their response was, 'I can't. I have this to do, or that to do.' These individuals were totally distracted by the lesser things they needed to do in life, and totally missed out on the God opportunity of a lifetime. It wasn't that their other duties were unimportant, nor were they to be neglected, but these individuals allowed the issues of life to take the place of God's call on their life. If we're not careful, we can justify the things that seem urgent as the reason why we can't fulfill our destiny.

When my husband and I were preparing to go to the mission field, it wasn't the big things that caused us to be distracted but the little things — which often became big things. What do we keep, what do we sell, what do we give away? Who is going to take care of the belongings we want to keep while we are gone, (for however long that is)? Who is willing to take our cat? Do we keep the car for visits or do we sell the car? How can we get everything done before we leave?

In saying YES to God, we have to be intentional about putting things in place to minimise those distractions, while at the same time, putting our trust in God's ability to have a solution for each one of those little things that take our eyes off the main event.

The Bible emphasises the importance of intentionality. It tells us the only way we will get ahead is to stay focused.

Keep looking straight ahead, without turning aside. Know where you are headed, and you will stay on solid ground. Don't make a mistake by turning to the right or the left. Proverbs 4:25-27 (CEV)

As a family we wrote a list of what we needed to attend to, then we put out the call and trusted God with the outcome. Many of our friends rallied around us and took care of all the things we had allowed our mind to be consumed with and overly concerned about.

If only those who Jesus called to follow Him had just trusted Him to take care of their other obligations and followed the call on their life. If they had, they would have discovered a God who is just as concerned about their duties as they were. I know it's a well-used phrase, but when you are taking care of God's business, He takes care of yours — and from experience, we know this to be true.

What does the Word of God say?

Instead, be concerned above everything else with the Kingdom of God and with what He requires of you, and He will provide you with all these other things.

Matthew 6:33 (GNT)

Don't worry about anything, but in all your prayers ask God for what you need, always asking Him with a thankful heart. And God's peace, which is far beyond human understanding, will keep your hearts and minds safe in union with Christ Jesus.

Philippians 4: 6–7 (GNT)

Questions

Q: What is one distraction you can identify in your life right now that's slowing down the process of you moving towards your God-given calling?

....
....
....
....

Q: What are you willing to do about it?

....
....
....
....

Now write a list of all the other distractions. The duties that need to be passed on or moved off your 'to do' list. Write down time wasters in your life (e.g., too much social media), and any negative influences.

**Anything that is grabbing your attention
and pulling you away from the main event
which is God's plan and purpose for your life,
is a distraction.**

....
....
....
....

....
....
....
....
....

Q: What do you need to do to make this process a reality?

....
....
....
....

Q: What do you need help with?

....
....
....
....

Q: Who can help you?

....
....
....
....

Day 3

LITTLE FLASK, BIG JARS

2 Kings 4:1–8 tells us the story of a women whose husband died and left her with a debt. Creditors were coming to take her two boys as payment. She cries out to the prophet Elisha for help. He asks her, 'What do you have in your house?'

'What do you have in your house', she was asked. We can sometimes overlook what is in our house (in our hands) as insignificant, believing it isn't enough for God to use to get our miracle. However, when God asks us this question, He has a miracle in mind. Although this widow looked at the small amount of oil in her house, she chose to believe that God could do something supernatural with it.

The woman tells him that all she has is a little flask of oil. Elisha instructs her to go and get as many empty jars as she can find and pour oil into each of the jars. When all the jars were full and there were no more jars left, the oil stopped flowing. Elisha then tells her to sell the oil, pay her debts and live on what is left.

This is a perfect example of how God can use the little we have to do more than we could possibly imagine. The widow was in a desperate situation. Not only was she unable to pay her debts, but the creditors were going to take her sons as payment. She could have looked at what she had in the natural and thought, 'What good can this do?' Instead, she trusted God to do something miraculous with what was in her hands. What she needed was enough to pay her creditors and keep her boys. However, because she chose the trust route, what she received was not only what she needed, but also enough to live on.

Although my family and I were not in the same position as this widow, before we left to serve overseas, we did need a miracle. We desperately needed to pay off the debts that had accumulated from the business we had bought that had stripped us of everything. To leave the shores of our own country and serve in another, we not only needed a clean slate, but money to live on. The only oil we had were our possessions — which we were selling.

We chose to trust God with what was in our hands — those few possessions — and watch God bless our 'oil'. I'm not kidding when I say, what began as an advertised 'one day' garage sale (yard sale), became an almost daily stream of people coming to buy things, that lasted for several weeks. As God sent people to buy, we would pour that 'oil' into jars that needed filling (our debt) and found we still had enough left over to live on. In the natural it didn't add up, but by putting our faith into action, we paid off our debt. We got our miracle.

Just as God filled our jars with oil, He will do it for you also. What's your oil? Begin pouring that oil as needed, and watch God refill your flask over and over again until there is not only enough for what you need, but also enough to live on.

What does the Word of God say?

This generous God who supplies abundant seed for the farmer, which becomes bread for our meals, is even more extravagant toward you. First he supplies every need, plus more. Then he multiplies the seed as you sow it, so that the harvest of your generosity will grow.

2 Corinthians 9:10 (TPT)

'Bring me another jar', she said to one of her sons. 'There aren't any more!' he told her. And then the olive oil stopped flowing. When she told the man of God what had happened, he said to her, 'Now sell the olive oil and pay your debts, and you and your sons can live on what is left over.

2 Kings 4:3 (NIV)

Questions

Q: What's in your hands right now that God can use and multiply to propel you into your God-given purpose?

....
....
....
....
....
....

**For the widow it was literally oil.
For us, it was possessions sitting in our garage.**

Q: What's your oil?

....
....
....
....
....
....

Q: What do you need to do to create that oil?

> The widow needed to collect jars and continue filling them until there were no more jars left. For us, we needed to continue opening our door to anyone who would come and buy our possessions.

……………………………………………………………………………………
……………………………………………………………………………………
……………………………………………………………………………………
……………………………………………………………………………………

Q: What's stopping you from getting the oil flowing?

……………………………………………………………………………………
……………………………………………………………………………………
……………………………………………………………………………………
……………………………………………………………………………………

Q: What can you do about that?

……………………………………………………………………………………
……………………………………………………………………………………
……………………………………………………………………………………
……………………………………………………………………………………

Day 4

FAITH OF A MUSTARD SEED

Matthew 17:20 tells us that if we have even just 'grain sized faith', He will do mighty things. I'm so grateful that God only requires a mustard seed of faith from us to move even the greatest of mountains — mountains in our lives which seem impossible for us to conquer. I asked God the question, 'Why do You require only a tiny morsel of faith from us to fulfil our seemingly monumental unachievable requests?' His answer was simple. 'Deb, I know so well your human frailty. The comparison between what you can believe for, compared to what I can do, is incomparable. My ability is infinite. My capability compared to your faith ability is immeasurable, but with that little you have, I am more than able to do what is needed to be done.' Isn't God amazing?

When we began our debt-busting journey, that 'debt mountain' was so big, we couldn't see any way of eliminating it. This monster seemed relentless in stopping us moving on to our next season. All we knew to do was offer up our mustard seed of faith to God, and continue moving forward, while listening to His voice for instructions about the next step.

This is key. Give what you have to God, keep moving forward, and keep your ears attuned to God's voice. Take it step by step. You don't ever get to where you're going in one giant leap.

As we combined that tiny mustard seed of faith with God's amazing capability, we saw that ugly big mountain supernaturally get cut down little by little, piece by piece. Then, all of a sudden, we saw that mountain get thrown deep into the sea. Our oversized monstrosity of a business debt was paid in full and in supernatural time. God really does move mountains!

You may have a mountain sitting in front of you right now that you believe is stopping you from fulfilling the call of God on your life, however God's Word tells us to trust Him with our mustard seed of faith. The Word tells us that moving forward one step at a time — doing what we can do in the natural — will lead to that mountain being hurled into the abyss.

I love this quote by Pope Benedict XVI. He says; ' I have a mustard seed; and I'm not afraid to use it.'

Pick up your mustard seed of faith and put it into action.

What does the Word of God say?

'You don't have enough faith,' Jesus told them. 'I tell you the truth, if you had faith even as small as a mustard seed, you could say to this mountain move from here to there, and it would move. Nothing would be impossible.'

Matthew 17:20 (NLT)

This is the confidence we have in approaching God: that if we ask anything according to His will, He hears us.

1 John 5:14 (NIV)

Your ears will hear a word behind you, 'This is the way, walk in it.' whenever you turn to the right or to the left.

Isaiah 30:21 (AMP)

Questions

Q: What's the mountain in front of you right now?

....
....
....
....

Q: What's your first response when you're faced with a mountain in your life?

....
....
....
....

Our history is a great teacher.

Q: Thinking about other mountains you've had in your life in the past, how did God come through for you then?

....
....
....

**Remember,
it's the same God, same authority,
just different mountain.**

Q: What do you need to lay at the altar in faith?

....
....
....
....

Q: What do you need to pick up in order to do something about it?

....
....
....
....

Be still and hear the voice of God speaking to you right now.

Q: What is He saying to you?

....
....
....
....
....

Day 5

SEVEN LOAVES, A FEW FISH AND FOUR THOUSAND MEN

I remember waking one particular morning before we moved overseas, to God's whisper. He reminded me of the unique and specific plans He had for both myself and my family. As I pondered all that entailed, it began to overwhelm me. I knew the population of the country we were going to was over 70 million — with insurmountable needs, both physically and spiritually.

In the natural, I couldn't begin to imagine how we could even meet a fraction of this huge population's needs. With a challenge of that magnitude before our family, I asked God to show me how He was going to use us. He led me to Matthew 15:32-39 (NLT) titled 'Jesus Feeds Four Thousand'. How appropriate I thought. We were going to need a Jesus solution to feed the millions in that nation — body, soul and spirit.

In Matthew 15:32-33, we see that Jesus felt sorry for the crowd because they had been with Him for three days and were now out of food. He didn't want to send them away hungry, but the disciples had no idea where they would get enough food for so many.

I could totally understand what the disciples were saying, as we were asking God this very thing. 'God where are we going to get enough skill, talent, time, money and resource, to 'feed' this huge crowd in this new land which you are showing us we will reach?'

Jesus said (to the disciples), 'How much bread do you have?' Disciples: 'Seven loaves, and a few small fish.' (v34)

Jesus was saying to me, 'What is in your hands now Deb?' My reply: 'Lord, I have a passion, I can speak, I can teach, I can play music, but is that going to be enough?'

Jesus to his disciples: 'Sit everyone down, I will take these loaves and fish, thank God for them, then break them into pieces and you will distribute them to the crowd.' (v 35-36)

Jesus said to me, 'Deb, sit down a minute. Now give me what you have. I will thank God for it, then break it into as many pieces as necessary, multiplying it for you to distribute to my people.'

The crowd ate and seven large baskets of leftover food were picked up. (v37)

Jesus reminded me that what was in my basket was more than enough. 'Give me what you have, and watch what I will do with it.' He told me.

The enemy will always tell you that you aren't good enough. That you don't have what it takes, or couldn't possibly do what God has in mind for you to do. However, God says, 'Not only have I chosen you, equipped you and appointed you, but I will multiply what you do for generations.'

What does the Word of God say?

Indeed, I will greatly bless you, and I will greatly multiply your seed as the stars of the heavens and as the sand which is on the seashore; and your seed shall possess the gate of their enemies.

Genesis 22:17 (NASB)

Then Jesus called his disciples and told them, 'I feel sorry for these people. They have been here with me for three days, and they have nothing left to eat. I don't want to send them away hungry, or they will faint along the way.' The disciples replied, 'Where would we get enough food here in the wilderness for such a huge crowd?' Jesus asked, 'How much bread do you have?' They replied, 'Seven loaves, and a few small fish.' So Jesus told all the people to sit down on the ground. Then he took the seven loaves and the fish, thanked God for them, and broke them into pieces. He gave them to the disciples, who distributed the food to the crowd. They all ate as much as they wanted. Afterward, the disciples picked up seven large baskets of leftover food. There were 4,000 men who were fed that day, in addition to all the women and children.

Matthew 15:32-38 (NLT)

Questions

Q: What is the dominant voice you are listening to?

....
....
....
....

Weigh it up against what God and His Word says about you.

....
....
....
....
....
....

Q: What gifts, talents, resource has God given you? Write them down.

....
....
....
....
....

**When God calls you,
He equips you with everything
you need for the task.**

Q: What is one gift, talent or resource you possess that you have used for God before?

....
....
....
....
....
....

Q: What was the outcome, the fruit borne from it?

....
....
....
....
....
....
....
....
....
....

Day 6

BUT I NEED THIS FOR LATER!

Proverbs 3:5–6 reminds us to trust in the Lord with all our heart and not to depend on our understanding: to seek His will in all we do and He will show us which path to take.

During out 'debt-busting' season, we had a bill to pay that was due the following week and, for a change, we already had the money in the bank for this one ahead of time. It was a nice feeling to have the money ready and waiting before it was due, instead of just on time. Don't get me wrong, I was always totally grateful for all the 'just on times' God had provided for, but I have to admit, this 'ahead of time' thing was more my style. I was feeling pretty relaxed about it and quite pleased with myself that we had this one covered. What I wasn't planning on, was another bill coming in which would be due before the one I had been prepared for.

As usual, I cried out to God, as I had become very apt at doing, 'God, we don't have the money for this one, what are we supposed to do?' No sooner had I finished my not so holy prayer, God spoke ever so calmly to me saying, 'Deb, you do have the money for it.' I promptly replied: 'Not the money for the Insurance bill Lord? Remember, I planned it in advance. It has been wisely kept. I am a good steward girl!' Again, God spoke, 'I thought you trusted me in all things Deb! All things, are all things. Use what is in your hands.'

All things are all things. Do we trust God with all things? You can tell God that you trust Him with your health, but do you trust Him with your future? Or, you say that you trust Him with your finance, but do you trust Him with your family? I know it is easier said than done, but we grieve God when we don't trust Him fully. Sometimes it's a day-by-day trust, even moment-by-moment, but trust we must. Whatever you need to trust God for — whether that be family, future, health or finance — choose trust, despite how you may feel.

Regardless of what my own thoughts were telling me at that time, I chose trust. I trusted in God's ability to provide for the bill that I had planned ahead for, knowing that God is always true to His Word.

As soon as we paid the amount that was due, peace came upon me. We still didn't know how we were going to pay the bill that was due the following week, but what we did know was God was going to come through, somehow.

Well, you guessed it. God did come through. Just days before the other bill was to be paid, an unexpected cheque arrived in our mailbox from someone who felt prompted to send us some money. How much do you think it was for? You guessed it — almost the identical amount that was on our invoice!

What God did for us, He will do for you.

What does the Word of God say?

For you are indeed God, and your words are truth; and you have promised me these good things.

2 Samuel 7:28 (TLB)

Trust in the Lord completely, and do not rely on your own opinions. With all your heart rely on Him to guide you, and He will lead you in every decision you make. Become intimate with Him in whatever you do, and He will lead you wherever you go.

Proverbs 3:5-6 (TPT)

Questions

Proverbs 3:5 tells us to trust in the Lord with all our heart and not lean on our own understanding.

My question to you is this, 'Is God the God of each area of your life?'

Maybe you fully trust Him with your health, but not your finances. Maybe you believe He will always come through for you with your family, but not your future. God is the same God you put your trust in, in one area as He is in the areas you find challenging to do so.

Write down the area/s you find easy to trust God in, then follow it with the area/s you struggle to trust God in. Look at them and speak to the areas you struggle in.

**Remember,
the God of the mountain
is the God of the valley.**

I trust God in ....

....

....

....

....

....

I struggle to trust God in ……………………………………………………

………………………………………………………………………………………

………………………………………………………………………………………

………………………………………………………………………………………

………………………………………………………………………………………

………………………………………………………………………………………

………………………………………………………………………………………

………………………………………………………………………………………

Are you willing to prove His faithfulness?

Q: If so, what steps are you going to take to allow Him to show you just how faithful He is?

………………………………………………………………………………………

………………………………………………………………………………………

………………………………………………………………………………………

………………………………………………………………………………………

………………………………………………………………………………………

………………………………………………………………………………………

………………………………………………………………………………………

………………………………………………………………………………………

RUNNING ON EMPTY

Corrie ten Boom once said that 'If the devil can't make you sin, he'll make you busy.'

I have often quoted something similar myself. 'The enemy is happy for you to be so busy, even doing God's work, that you burn out.' Get to burn out and he has won. You are now no good for anyone.

At this junction, I believe it's important to bring this point up because unless you stay refuelled on your journey, your mind will take precedence over your spirit and you'll begin to look at what can't be done instead of what God can and will do through you.

You may be looking at how far you've come, or rather how far you still have to go, and think, 'I need to push this journey along.' What happens then is you begin to worry and get stressed out. You start running ahead of what God is wanting to do in you, to prepare you for what He has in store for you. And you miss out on the lesson, the stretching, the equipping He is doing in you, to be able to work through you.

Tell me where in the Word of God do you read, 'Then Jesus ran to the next town because He told everyone, "Hey I only have three and a half years to do this gig!"' Nowhere, right! You find Him resting, getting away with His Father to pray, and even when urgent needs came His way — waiting. From that position, miracles took place, lessons were taught, revelation was revealed, and His prophetic voice was proclaimed.

Why then, do we think we should do any different? Why do so many of us seem to believe self-care will take care of itself? Self-care is just that: caring for self. If we are not healthy — body, soul and spirit — how can we pour out to others in a healthy balanced way?

Rushing or getting busy doesn't equate to fruitfulness. We get pulled in every direction because of need and then we become overwhelmed or worn out. We do this not because we want to wear ourselves out, but often because we care about others so much. We want to be selfless, so we go the extra mile. The question we need to consider is, 'Are we pouring out of a full or an empty vessel?'

If you don't plan your time, your time will plan you. If you don't care for yourself, everything else will take a piece of you, until you have nothing left to give and find yourself giving out of an empty tank — a tank empty of energy, clear thinking and motivation.

What does the Word of God say?

Are you tired? Worn out? Burned out on religion? Come to me. Get away with me and you'll recover your life. I'll show you how to take a real rest. Walk with me and work with me — watch how I do it. Learn the unforced rhythms of grace. I won't lay anything heavy or ill-fitting on you. Keep company with me and you'll learn to live freely and lightly.

Matthew 11:28–30 (MSG)

Don't burn out; keep yourselves fueled and aflame. Be alert servants of the Master...

Romans 12:11 (MSG)

Questions

Q: What are you doing to safeguard against getting depleted in your spirit, emotions, health, time, relationships and mind?

....

....

....

....

Take stock of how much time you are putting in to refuelling.

Write in the columns where you are doing well and where you need to improve.

BALANCED (doing well)	**UNBALANCED** (need to improve)

Q: Now that you have recognised the areas of weakness (not failures), how can you begin to strengthen those areas?

For example, if time is unbalanced, consider who or what is robbing you of time? I am not talking about things that are important to your wellbeing, like recreational time, but time that is being lost or wasted that you know should be used in a more productive way.

Take stock of your day, week and month. Think through each area. Don't rush this, because it's important for you to move forward in a healthy, balanced way.

....
....
....
....
....
....
....
....
....
....
....
....
....
....
....
....

Reflection Time

LET'S TAKE A MOMENT TO REFLECT ON HOW FAR YOU'VE COME

Firstly, congratulations on getting this far. You are one third of the way through this devotional.

Score Yourself

If you were to give yourself a score out of 10 (10 being the best scenario), where are you sitting at this point?

1. I know I have some work to do.
5. I'm getting there.
10. I'm right where I need to be.

DON'T RISK YOUR DESTINY - I've taken steps to begin my journey.

1 2 3 4 5 6 7 8 9 10

THOSE LITTLE DISTRACTIONS - I'm staying focused on the things that matter.

1 2 3 4 5 6 7 8 9 10

LITTLE FLASKS, BIG JARS - I've identified my 'oil' for God to multiply.

1 2 3 4 5 6 7 8 9 10

FAITH OF A MUSTARD SEED - I'm laying my mountains at God's alter.

1   2   3   4   5   6   7   8   9   10

SEVEN LOAVES, A FEW FISH AND FOUR THOUSAND MEN - I'm giving God my all to use.

1   2   3   4   5   6   7   8   9   10

BUT I NEED THIS FOR LATER - I'm learning to trust God in all areas.

1   2   3   4   5   6   7   8   9   10

RUNNING ON EMPTY - I'm working on keeping my tank full.

1   2   3   4   5   6   7   8   9   10

For the areas you are moving forward in, give yourself a high five and celebrate. For the areas you need to adjust, don't beat yourself up, but instead, congratulate yourself for being honest in identifying them.

Be encouraged by the fact that working on life disciplines take time. Make the necessary adjustments and move forward.

Part II
Strength Builders

Day 8

ATTITUDE

When my husband and I were attending a mission college to prepare us for cross-cultural life, we had to live on a very strict budget. In our quest for cheap meals, Paul and I discovered 99 cent lasagnes at a local supermarket. These little gems became our daily staple as they managed to fill our stomachs and match our budget. We would share one at lunchtime and take one home for dinner. We were a little embarrassed about eating our 99 cent lasagne in front of our hosts, so we always waited until they were well and truly finished with their own dinner and away from the dining table before we would go and heat up our humble meal.

We would often come home to their table laid out and dressed for their evening meal. What would it be tonight? Roast dinner, Italian spaghetti, sausages and vegetables or a hearty soup? Whatever they were serving up, it always smelled divine. Our stomachs would ache as our taste buds went into overdrive, screaming with desire for what they were having. Sometimes they'd ask us if we would like to dine with them but we always declined, saying we had our own meal sorted. We'd thank them before escaping to our bedroom. We couldn't afford the further $100 per week we'd been told it would cost for them to feed us, so we used the time they ate their meal to dive into our mission studies. After they had well and truly finished their dinner, we would take a break to 'feast' on our own special meal.

One particular night, as we arrived home, we walked through the front door with lasagne in hand and headed towards our bedroom as usual. We had hardly reached the doorway of our bedroom when we were called to the kitchen. 'We would like to invite you for dinner,' our hosts said.

We assumed they meant, 'We can feed you for a fee if you like', and again, we thanked them and said we were okay, that we had something for dinner. However, tonight they weren't buying our 'We are okay' story. 'Paul and Deb, we're not asking you join us as boarders, but as our guests; no money. You can save your lasagne for another night.'

I wanted to cry. We had tried so hard to hide our little secret, but somehow, they just knew. We thanked them profusely and for the first time, sat with our host family to enjoy the best meal we'd had since arriving in Sydney. This night was to become the first of many nights they would set a place for Paul and I, inviting us to join them.

From that day on, we not only received free meals each day from our hosts, but they also welcomed our kids to stay with us for free.

Attitude is everything. It comes back to the glass half full or glass half empty perspective. We could have complained about the fact we were the only ones in our college course who had to survive on 99 cent meals each day. We could have complained that we only got to see our family occasionally. We could have complained that while others went to the movies, ate out at restaurants and bought things, we had to go straight home, and lock ourselves behind closed doors with our small meal. We could have complained about others getting benefits to help them get through college while we hadn't been accepted for any allowance at all. But thank God, we chose the glass half full attitude, and praised Him for feeling full on our mini meals, for providing free morning and afternoon tea, and giving us a comfortable bed to sleep in each night. We stayed appreciative to God for the willing friends who took care of our beautiful kids 160km away so we could complete our studies, and remained grateful to God as He showered unexpected provision on us in ways we could never have imagined.

Attitude will make or break you, and others will also notice how you react or respond to situations in your life. It's not just God who takes note of it, but those around you also. I believe keeping our attitude sweet was one of the reasons why our host family began to include us in their family life.

What does the Word of God say?

Go, eat your food with gladness, and drink your wine with a joyful heart, for God has already approved what you do.

Ecclesiastes 9:7 (NIV)

Finally, brothers and sisters, whatever is true, whatever is noble, whatever is right, whatever is pure, whatever is lovely, whatever is admirable — if anything is excellent or praiseworthy — think about such things.

Philippians 4:8 (NIV)

Questions

Q: How is your attitude meter looking?

It's easy to look at what others have while you're wading through muddy waters. Take another look. Change your 'glasses' and you'll find that there is life in those streams. There is always something to be grateful for during those seasons. God rewards a grateful heart.

Write down what you are grateful for in this season.

....
....
....
....
....
....
....
....
....
....
....
....
....
....
....

Day 9

HUMILITY

A partner to attitude is humility.

I think one of the most encouraging things to experience when you're on your own journey through life is to listen to the stories of other people's journeys, glean from their experiences and take on board any wise advice they may have. Staying teachable and humble spirited will actually launch us further in our own walk when we choose to do this.

I learnt this lesson very early on when I was speaking at a women's conference in the north of the state of Tasmania. I was privileged to share the stage with a well-known, world-class speaker. After one of the meetings, we sat down together and she began asking me lots of questions about family and how I kept our family healthy while doing ministry. I couldn't believe a seasoned speaker who had a large ministry of her own, was asking me these questions. Although I was able to answer her questions, I had to ask her why she, being so advanced in ministry, was interested in my perspective on these things. She told me something I'll never forget. She said, 'Wherever I go and whoever I meet, I try to learn something from people I engage with so I continue to grow. I always want to remain a learner, as I believe we can all learn from each other.'

Had I not learnt this important lesson from that seasoned speaker, I could have missed out on valuable insight due to, (I am ashamed to say), being judgmental about who I thought would be good to learn from and who would not.

One evening, several weeks after that women's conference, my husband and I attended a meeting where we were to hear from a man who had lived and served overseas for a period of time. We knew this person well in his role as a Bible school lecturer, and although he was a lovely man, he spoke in a quiet, monotone voice. Knowing this about him, it would've been easy for me to form the opinion that he was boring and therefore a waste of time to listen to. Thankfully, I was saved by that well-known pastor who had spoken wisdom into my life.

Rather than thinking pridefully, that I couldn't possibly gain any interesting information from this man, I instead chose to lean in. I gained a wealth of knowledge as he shared story after story of his experiences and the lessons he'd learnt around navigating life on foreign soil. It was gold.

We know the saying; 'Don't judge a book by its cover,' or in this case by a pre-conceived idea. You never know who you'll meet, or who is already in your world, who will teach you something that will be pure gold for you to take on board. It could very well be the missing piece in your puzzle. Keep learning. Keep listening.

What does the Word of God say?

Consider carefully what you hear,' he continued. 'With the measure you use, it will be measured to you — and even more.

Mark 4:24 (NIV)

Whatever you have learned or received or heard from me, or seen in me — put it into practice. And the God of peace will be with you.

Philippians 4:9 (NIV)

Therefore encourage one another and build each other up, just as in fact you are doing.

1 Thessalonians 5:11 (NIV)

Questions

Q: Who's someone you can glean from who has already been on the journey you're embarking on? Who's in your world that can bring clarity to your situation? Who can you learn from?

Write a list.

....
....
....
....
....
....
....
....

Now that you have your list, write some questions down that you're seeking answers for.

....
....
....
....
....

Work on making appointments with these people. If it's someone you know or you want to get to know, call them and connect. If it's someone you don't know, who is outside of your sphere of influence, make time to listen to their podcast, watch their YouTube video, or read their book/s.

Get out your schedule and take action now.

Day 10

PRAISE

Attitude and humility go hand in hand, however, praise is the third spoke in the wheel. Praise moves the heart of God. Praise is not third in line, but we have to adjust our attitude and be humble in spirit in order to praise God for the right reasons. We cannot praise God just for the purpose of getting something, but must praise Him for who He is. Praise Him for being the King of Kings. Praise Him for being the Lord of Lords. Praise Him for being the authority above every other power. Praise Him for being the magnificent creator of all things. Praise Him for being the great lover of our soul. Praise Him for all He has done for us. Praise Him that He has His hand on us and has chosen us to be His own.

As human beings, it's our natural default to enter God's throne room with our requests. 'God help me do this.' 'I need that.' 'What are you doing?' I'm still guilty of this myself in my own walk with God; I would be lying if I said I wasn't. However, I'm more conscious of when I'm doing it these days — for example, when I find myself rushing into His throne room with my list.

I remember waking one morning with a conviction in my spirit about how I was approaching God so often this way in my prayer time. The Holy Spirit was putting His finger on me to bring awareness to the way I was so often approaching God. I needed to reconsider what my conversations with God were like. It wasn't as if I didn't love Him, praise Him and worship Him, but I had to admit that most of the time I praised Him for what He was doing for me rather than who He was.

It takes conscious awareness on our part to form the daily habit of just being in His presence. It's so easy to get caught up in our needs that we forget just to be still before Him. 'Be still and know that I am God.' Psalm 46:10, (NIV). God is waiting for each of us to just sit at His feet. Sit in His presence and hear His voice. Praise Him for who He is. When we do this, God will respond by revealing more of Himself to us, and we'll gain a greater revelation of all He is, and who He is in all His fulness. It's here we gain a new perspective on His ability to answer our requests.

Rick Warren says there are 7 benefits to praise:

Praise lifts your spirit	Psalm 42:5-6 (NLT)
Praise helps you sense God's presence	Psalm 140:13 (NIV)
Praise enlarges your perception of God	Psalm 69:30 (AMP)
Praise reveals solutions we can't see	Psalm 73:16-17 (NCV)
Praise helps us remember God's blessing	Psalm 105:1, 5 (MSG)
Praise enlists God's protection	2 Chronicles 20 (NIV)
Praise breaks chains and opens doors	Acts 16:26 (NLT)

What does the Word of God say?

The one thing I want from God, the thing I seek most of all, is the privilege of meditating in his Temple, living in his presence every day of my life, delighting in his incomparable perfections and glory.

Psalm 27:4 (TLB)

But as for me, I get as close to him as I can! I have chosen him, and I will tell everyone about the wonderful ways He rescues me.

Psalm 73:28 (TLB)

Humble yourselves before the Lord, and He will lift you up.

James 4:10 (NIV)

Questions

Forming a habit of praise takes practice.

Write down what you want to praise God for to help you make the conscious decision to begin your time with God from that place.

**Be still and know that I am God.
Psalm 46:10 (NIV).**

In His presence He will reveal Himself to you, and what He desires you to know about Him and His ability.

Still your heart and then write down what He is saying to you.

....
....
....
....
....
....
....
....

Q: How has your perspective changed on His ability to meet your needs now?

....
....
....
....
....
....
....

Day 11

JOY

The joy of the Lord is your strength and your stronghold. Nehemiah 8:10b (AMP)

A happy heart is good medicine and a joyful mind causes healing. Proverbs 17:22 (AMP)

If God's joy is our strength, and a happy heart brings healing to our bodies, it makes sense to embrace this attribute. It will be profitable for each area of our lives; body, soul and spirit.

The question is, 'How do we find joy in the midst of challenges? When life throws twists and turns at us that we are not expecting, how do we stay strong, as the scripture implies?'

The truth is, in life, there will always be situations, challenges, circumstances or even excuses we make, which attempt to prevent us from living a life of joy.

You have probably heard people say things like; 'When I have no problems in my life, I will be happy.' 'When I finish college, I will be able to get on with my life.' 'When I get married, I will be content.' 'When I have kids, then my life will be fulfilled.' 'When I am rich, then I can give to the poor.' 'When I have my house just as I want it, then I can do ministry, business, have a hobby.' 'When everything is running smoothly in my life, then I can think about my life's passion and calling.'

The "When I..." mindset can rob us of our now, if we are not mindful of it.

Sure, in times of struggle and challenges, we can all wonder how we can rise above it, but I want to say, that even in these times, we can. I can testify to that fact.

Personally, my husband and I have had, and continue to have, challenges that can stop us in our tracks. What I have learnt over the years though is the enemy knows where we're weak, so he will come and attack us in that space and try and give us a narrative that produces fear and doubt in our lives. If we're not aware of this, the enemy's voice will speak louder to us than the voice of reason and truth.

Joy is not the same as happiness. Joy is founded in God's faithfulness to deliver us, guide us, protect us and see us through to the other side. Happiness is always dependent on how we feel or what is happening in our lives. Joy is strength — God strength. Happiness wavers.

Joy is found in the knowledge that no matter what's going on in or around us, we can continue to walk in victory, peace, contentment, and yes, even joy. Why? Because God is faithful to His finished work. What refocuses me personally, is looking back at each past circumstance and remembering His faithfulness. He conquered every challenge and defeated every foe then, and because 'He is the same yesterday, today and forever,' Hebrews 13:8 (NIV) He will do it again.

There's so much to experience in your every day. Don't miss it. Take your eyes off the mountain/obstacle/problem in front of you and focus on the God of the mountain and of the valley.

You will show me the path that leads to life; your presence fills me with joy and brings me pleasure forever. Psalm 16:11 (GNT)

What does the Word of God say?

But let all who take refuge and put their trust in You rejoice. Let them ever sing for joy; Because You cover and shelter them. Let those who love Your name be joyful and exult in You.

Psalm 5:11 (AMP)

You will show me the path of life; In Your presence is fullness of joy; In Your right hand there are pleasures forevermore.

Psalm 16:11 (AMP)

You [O God] will increase the nation, You, will multiply their joy; They will rejoice before You like the joy and jubilation of the harvest. As men rejoice when they divide the spoil [of victory].

Isaiah 9:3 (AMP)

May the God of hope fill you with all joy and peace in believing [through the experience of your faith] that by the power of the Holy Spirit you will abound in hope and overflow with confidence in His promises.

Romans 15:13 (AMP)

Questions

Q: What has caused you to lack joy?

....

....

....

....

....

....

**Happiness is always dependent on how we feel
or what is happening in our lives.
Joy is founded in God's faithfulness.**

Q: Understanding this truth, what are some 'Joy Statements' you could write to remind you of this truth?

For example: Joy comes through knowing my identity in Christ.

....

....

....

....

....

....

Q: Knowing that the joy of the Lord gives you strength, and it is not dependent on your circumstances, what steps will you take to move from a "When I..." mindset to an "I will..." mindset?

....
....
....
....
....
....
....
....
....
....
....
....

Remember, as you continue to pursue what God has put on your life, you can rest assured, knowing He is the same God who brought you through in the past, will be the same God who brings you through in the future.

Exchange a "When I..." statement with an "I will..." declaration.

Here are two examples:

Example 1: When I have time, then I can think about my life's passion and calling.

Exchange with one or both of these declarations:
- I will prioritise my schedule to research my passion / my calling.
- I will get in touch with someone who can help me begin the journey of my passion / my calling.

Example 2: When I get over the negative relationship with my friend that is consuming my thoughts, then I can think about my future.

Exchange with one or more of these declarations:
- I will trust you to work this situation out.
- I will bring this to your throne room and listen for your guidance and wisdom.
- I will have faith in Your ability to work out the best outcome.
- I will get some guidance from a trusted friend or counsellor so I can move forward.

Write your personal "When I..." and "I will..."

When I ....

....

....

I will ....

....

....

**Joy is a journey.
It starts with praise.**

Praise God for what He is doing in your life now. Praise Him for the seen and unseen that He's working on. Allow the voice of God's Word and truth to ring louder than the voice of the accuser.

Write your praise points down here.

....
....
....
....
....
....
....
....
....
....

Write down what you're enjoying about your journey so far.

....
....
....
....
....

Day 12

TRUST

I was attending a meeting many years ago where a world-renowned motivational speaker, Zig Ziglar, was the keynote speaker. I recall him saying that it takes a good 17 times to believe and act on something you have been told. He said that at first you hear it, and it's simply information that passes between your two ears. Then the next few times you hear it, it becomes a familiar message that sounds like a good idea. After that, your ears prick up and you listen more intently because it's starting to make sense to you. You even believe this is a good idea — for someone else. Eventually, you begin to take notice of what is being said as something that you need for yourself, but it isn't until around the seventeenth time that you consciously pick it up and put it into practice.

Over the past few days, you've learnt about the importance of attitude, humility and praise. It's easy to take what you've read and know it's both good and noteworthy, however it's another thing to believe it for yourself and put it into action. If you don't, those gems you receive will just end up gathering dust. You don't want to do that. Build that habit you began in yesterday's devotion.

Habits come in all forms. Changing how we behave takes habit also. To truly thrive in our journey with God and be used by God to produce His lasting fruit, we have to make sure we're not carrying bags we were never meant to carry.

I held a black belt in worry for a long time. I believed it was my job to rescue, protect and defend everyone in my world. This came about from taking on responsibilities as a child that I thought were mine to carry. I would get up in the morning and put my clothes on, along with my cloak of worry. Often, in my 'good intentional' way, I would fight battles for others that were not necessarily mine to fight. I would end up weary and the end result wasn't always positive.

I always knew Jesus was our burden carrier. I knew His Word was truth. I often prayed and committed the 'worry list' to God, but I constantly found myself picking up the 'burden pack' again on my way back out of God's throne room.

It wasn't until I was still and allowed God to minister His truth deep down in my spirit did it become a revelation. I had to become still to know that He is God. He is God, not me. It was in that stillness that God spoke these words to me, 'Deb, who told you that you are the burden carrier? That is my portfolio, not yours. You need to hand that over to me if you want to see real results and be released of the self-endorsed title you have given yourself.'

It took time to form the habit of handing over what only God could carry. Was it easy? Not at all. Many times, I would hand my burdens over to God, only to snatch them back as I walked out His door. Eventually, I learnt to leave my burdens at His feet and not pick them up again. I chose to build a habit of surrender and by doing that, I moved from just having the knowledge of God being my burden carrier, to a conviction in my Spirit that God could be trusted with my concerns.

What does the Word of God say?

Come to me, all you who are weary and burdened, and I will give you rest. Take my yoke upon you and learn from me, for I am gentle and humble in heart, and you will find rest for your souls. For my yoke is easy and my burden is light.

Matthew 11: 28-30 (NIV)

I am allowed to do all things, but not all things are good for me to do. I am allowed to do all things, but I will not let anything make me its slave.

1 Corinthians 6:12 (NCV)

Questions

Q: What are you carrying that you know needs to be given to God?

....
....
....
....
....
....
....
....

Q: What habits do you need to form and which ones do you need to release?

....
....
....
....
....
....
....
....

Q: Now you're aware of what you need to put into your life and what you need to release, what action will you begin today — and every day from now on — to form a healthy habit?

....
....
....
....
....
....
....
....
....
....
....
....

This devotional is a 21-day devotional on purpose. It takes 21 days to begin to change a habit — 66 days for a habit to become behavioural according to studies taken at the University College of London. (See reference in appendix). Be consistent with the changes for at least 21 days and you'll find the following days will become easier. Check in with those you've chosen to be accountable to.

Day 13

TRACTION

Have you ever owned one of those little toy cars where, in order for them to move forward, you need to pull them backward? These cars need tension on their mechanics, otherwise they can't move forward. The greater the tension placed on them, the greater their speed and the farther they go.

When our son was young, he owned many of these cars. He loved them. He would line them up in a row and then, one by one, pull those little cars back as far as they would go, before releasing them down our narrow hallway. He knew that the more tension he created in pulling those little cars back, the more momentum they would gain and the further they would go. The thrill and satisfaction of knowing he had created that momentum in those cars caused him to want to get up, make his way down the hall to retrieve each one, and do it all over again. With great anticipation, he would watch them fly down his 'racetrack' in the hope that this time, they would go just a little farther than the time before.

Momentum is defined as 'the force that keeps an object moving; once you push it, it keeps going under its own momentum' (Cambridge Dictionary). Momentum, however, doesn't just happen. Momentum occurs when there has been a period of pull back to cause tension before something is released. It's not negative tension, but stretching tension.

You'll find as you journey through these 21 days, there will be times of tension. It may feel like you're being pulled back instead of moving forward. It's during those times you'll get frustrated with yourself and with God. 'Why is this happening Lord?' you might ask. 'I'm doing everything you asked me to do. Why is it so hard?' When these times come, the question is not, 'Why is this happening Lord?' But rather, 'What are you teaching me right now Lord, that is going to be beneficial to propel me farther ahead?'

Often during those tension times, God is trying to get your attention. Just like those little cars are meant to be pulled back and held in position for a moment in time to produce their best performance when released, God pulls you back so He can prepare you for what's coming up next. Don't despise the tension. It's in that place where you will dig deep wells with God. Listen to His voice and open your heart to receive His Word for your next step.

Take time to praise Him for who He is, not what He can do for you. You don't want to miss this holy tension time. This is the place God reveals more of Himself to you — things which you didn't know before. It will be pure gold. When God sees that you're fully immersed in what He has pulled you back for, He's going to release you to use the gems He's spoken into your spirit, taking you farther than you thought you would ever go.

What does the Word of God say?

But those who trust in the Lord will become strong again. They will be like eagles that grow new feathers. They will run and not get weak. They will walk and not get tired.

Isaiah 40:31 (ERV)

This is why I wait upon you, expecting your breakthrough, for your Word brings me hope.

Psalm 130:5 (TPT)

Be still and know that I am God.

Psalm 46:10 (NIV)

Questions

Q: Are you in the tension zone at the moment? If so, don't resist it, but allow God to speak to you. Write down what He's saying to you.

....
....
....
....
....
....
....
....

Q: If you are not in this tension zone at the moment, but have experienced it in the past, how did you respond to it?

....
....
....
....
....
....

Q: What have you learnt through today's devotion about tension and momentum?

....
....
....
....
....
....
....
....

Day 14

GOD'S PLATFORM

We've just read about the purpose of tension. Now we're going to look at God's timing for those doors we've been waiting on to open.

In our eagerness to see things happen as quickly as we'd like, we often try to push doors open that aren't ready to be unlocked. When we allow God to do the door opening, however, doors will fling wide open.

Trying to do something in our own strength, leaving God out of the picture, is like cutting James 2:22 in half, which says, 'You see that his faith and his actions were working together and his faith was made complete by what he did' (NIV). It cannot be just works, it must always be coupled with faith; trusting and leaning on God and His timing. If God is calling us, He will stamp us with His authority, and that God authority will always make a way for us.

Our job is to look for the signs. Watch for the opportunities. Position ourselves. Stay alert and be prepared to move with our bags packed when those doors open up to us.

I remember when Paul and I were fundraising for our long-term overseas ministry. Although we were known in the state we were living in, we weren't known well enough to stand on a big platform to share our vision. Raising funds for long-term overseas ministry takes a lot of work and we were doing everything we knew to do, however it wasn't going to get us to our destiny in the timeframe we believed God had given us. God told us to be ready, to be available and to look for the signs and opportunities He would open up to us. It would've been easy to try and push doors that we had no authority to push, however, we knew we needed to wait on God's timing.

My husband Paul often met with the then State President of our church movement, Ron, to chat about general church business. Our State Pastor's Conference was coming up, so Paul wanted to catch up with Ron before he left for the conference. As Paul got up to leave, Ron said to Paul, 'You need to come to our State Pastor's Conference to share your vision with everyone. As a state, we should support you, and as a state, we should send you out.' Just like that, we went from being somewhat unknown to having a red-carpet invitation.

We could have tried to push on that door in our own strength, in our own way and in our own timing, but God in His true form set things up for us even before we asked. More than likely God had spoken to that pastor even before my husband attended their meeting. He unlocked a door that we thought was not possible to open.

The unlocking of the door was a surprise, however, us being prepared was key. We'd been preparing for a long time about what we would say when the opportunity arose to share on such a platform. God set things up for us, but we had to be prepared.

Whether you are waiting on the sign posts for a job promotion, a ministry opportunity, a relationship to form, for a shift in your circumstances, or simply for what could possibly be next, get equipped, get prepared and ready yourself.

What does the Word of God say?

Ask the LORD your God for a sign, whether in the deepest depths or in the highest heights.

Isaiah 7:11 (NIV)

This is the message from the One who is holy and true, the One who has the key of David. What He opens, no one can close; and what He closes, no one can open.

Revelation 3:7 (NLT)

Questions

Q: What area/s of life do you need to grow in, to be ready?

> Even if you don't know your next step, invest in personal growth.

....
....
....
....
....
....
....
....

Q: What doors have you been trying to open in your own strength? In your own timing?

> These doors are not necessarily wrong doors, but it's possibly not the right time.

....
....
....
....
....

When we're waiting on certain doors to open, we can't just sit and wait, we have to prepare. We need to be armed and ready.

Q: What do you need to do to ready yourself? This can be anything from decluttering your home to preparing a message to share with the world.

Make a list and get started, because when the doors open, you want to be fully equipped.

…………………………………………………………………………………

…………………………………………………………………………………

…………………………………………………………………………………

…………………………………………………………………………………

…………………………………………………………………………………

…………………………………………………………………………………

…………………………………………………………………………………

…………………………………………………………………………………

…………………………………………………………………………………

…………………………………………………………………………………

…………………………………………………………………………………

…………………………………………………………………………………

…………………………………………………………………………………

…………………………………………………………………………………

…………………………………………………………………………………

…………………………………………………………………………………

Reflection Time

LET'S TAKE A MOMENT TO REFLECT ON HOW FAR YOU'VE COME

Firstly, congratulations on getting this far. You are two thirds of the way through this devotional. If you were to give yourself a score out of 10 (10 being the best scenario), where are you sitting at this point?

Score Yourself

1. I know I have some work to do.
5. I'm getting there.
10. I'm right where I need to be.

ATTITUDE - I'm choosing to see God's provision during hard seasons.

1   2   3   4   5   6   7   8   9   10

HUMILITY - I'm learning to glean from others.

1   2   3   4   5   6   7   8   9   10

PRAISE - I'm practicing stillness in God's present and praising Him for who He is.

1   2   3   4   5   6   7   8   9   10

JOY - I'm exchanging "When I..." for "I will..." declarations.

1   2   3   4   5   6   7   8   9   10

TRUST - I'm trading worry for trust, what I pick up and what I lay down.

1   2   3   4   5   6   7   8   9   10

TRACTION - I'm committing the tension time to God because He is preparing me.

1   2   3   4   5   6   7   8   9   10

GOD'S PLATFORM - I'm readying myself for when God opens doors.

1   2   3   4   5   6   7   8   9   10

For the areas you are moving forward in, give yourself a high five and celebrate. For the areas you need to adjust, don't beat yourself up, but instead, congratulate yourself for being honest in identifying them.

Remember, working on life disciplines take time. Make the necessary adjustments and move forward.

Part III

Tools for Your Journey

Day 15

TOOL NUMBER ONE: Body

If you're going to make it to your God-given destination, you need to take a toolkit. These next seven days, the final week of our 21 days, is where you get packing with the essentials for your journey. This essential tool kit is made up of three parts: body, soul and spirit.

Surprise, surprise, we're not only spiritual beings, but we are physical and emotional beings also. We are body, we are soul and we are spirit. For us to be running on all our cylinders, we can't ignore any of these areas of our life. We were created by God to live fully alive and reach our destination in a healthy state, not limp to our promised land.

Your body has everything to do with your physical health. Your soul is all about your reasoning — your will and your emotions. Your spirit is your belief system (your worldview) which drives you on your chosen path. What you put into each of these components makes up the person you are today.

The Bible tells us that God created us in His image. He created our bodies, and that our bodies are the dwelling place of the Holy Spirit. I don't know about you, but being reminded of that fact was a wake-up call to me. Am I really caring for the body God created for me? Do I look after this vehicle that God's spirit dwells in? My body is a representative of whose I am, God's child.

This changed the narrative for me — from being obsessed with body image and weight to simply being the healthy person God intended me to be.

Have you thought much about this?

Taking care of our body has many benefits, both spiritual and physical.

- It's honouring to God. It tells Him that we're grateful for the way He created us so magnificently.
- It rewards us with the stamina to stay strong to fulfil God's calling on our life.
- It causes us to wake in the morning with a positive 'can do' perspective.
- It models to others, the importance of living healthy.

When we keep these things in mind, we'll strive to look after this temple in which the Holy Spirit dwells.

What does the Word of God say?

So, God created mankind in his own image, in the image of God he created them; male and female he created them.

Genesis 1:27 (NIV)

Don't you know that you yourselves are God's temple and that God's Spirit dwells in your midst?

1 Corinthians 3:16 (NIV)

Do you not know that your body is a temple of the Holy Spirit within you, whom you have from God? You are not your own, for you were bought with a price. So, glorify God in your body.

1 Corinthians 6: 19-20 (ESV)

Questions

Q: What comes to mind when you read this Scripture?

> Do you not know that your body is a temple of the Holy Spirit within you, whom you have from God? You are not your own, for you were bought with a price. So, glorify God in your body.
> 1 Corinthians 6:19-20 (ESV)

....
....
....
....
....
....
....
....
....
....
....
....
....
....
....

Q: Ask yourself this question as you read the following Scripture: Do I get enough sleep?

If not, or at times have restless sleep, what is it that keeps me up at night, and how can I apply this Word to my life?

> I can lie down at night and sleep soundly because You Lord, will keep me safe. Psalm 4:8 (CEV)

....

....

....

....

....

....

....

....

....

....

....

....

....

....

....

Each of us at times deal with challenges that come our way and affect our bodies.

> Sometimes it's a simple ailment, sometimes more serious. I suffer from fibromyalgia so for me to recover when my condition is causing me too much pain, I must stop, and I must rest. I find that difficult because I'm task orientated by nature. I remind myself that the enemy doesn't want us on top of our game, so he makes us feel guilty when we need rest.

Q: Are you looking after your body? What do you need to do, to the best of your ability, to care for the body God gave you so that you can serve Him well?

....
....
....
....
....
....

> We can often neglect taking care of ourselves when there's so much to get done. We just want to be on our way and step out into all that God has for us. If we don't stay strong, we are not able to give our best to others.

> For those of you who have flown on a plane, you would've heard one of the flight crew say; 'If pressure decreases, a mask will drop from the panel above. If you are travelling with children, put the mask on yourself first, then on the child.' Why? Because the adult needs enough breath in their lungs to have enough energy to help the child. It is the same for you. To step into all that God has for you, you need to be at your best. Your toolkit needs to be packed with a healthy you.

Day 16

TOOL NUMBER TWO: Soul

For as he thinks in his heart, so is he. Proverbs 23:7 (AMP)

In other words, 'What goes in, will come out.'

How true this is. Just like taking care of our body is important, healthy thinking is good for our soul, giving us strength to direct our focus on right, good and honourable things.

Our mind is consistently taking in information both consciously and subconsciously. If we aren't aware of what's going into our mind, our thought life can become clouded with negativity. We speak out of what we feed on. I know for myself, when negative thoughts consume my mind, or I have spoken badly to someone, it leaves me feeling heavy hearted. How about you? How often have you had negative thoughts towards someone, or worse still, towards yourself? How many times have you said to yourself, 'I wish I could take that back!'

Stinking thinking comes from feeding on bad fruit. None of us would consciously eat rotten fruit. If we had the choice between fly-infested produce and a sweet succulent peach, it's easy to guess what we would choose. What we feed on will affect our attitude, our mood, and even our body language. Immersing ourselves in an environment where gossip is continually festering about people will not produce a healthy mind. Social media, television programs and movies influence our mind. What fruit are you gaining from what you watch and read?

I'm not saying don't watch movies, television shows or engage with social media. Nor am I saying to wrap yourself in a bubble to protect yourself from the less than perfect environments that are around you.

We all have to deal with destructive influences daily, however what I'm saying is this: unless you're aware of your own weaknesses, it's easy to succumb to the temptation of filling your thought life with the bad rather than the good, which can keep you negatively bound.

There is good news. When we build a healthy defence force by feeding our mind with what is fruitful and profitable, we guard our hearts against arrows that are damaging to our soul.

We continually need to check the environment that we're growing in so we run our race mentally strong.

In the questions section, consider your answers from where you see yourself at the moment.

What does the Word of God say?

Above all else, guard your heart, for everything you do flows from it.

Proverbs 4:23 (NIV)

Finally, brothers and sisters, whatever is true, whatever is noble, whatever is right, whatever is pure, whatever is lovely, whatever is admirable — if anything is excellent or praiseworthy — think about such things.

Philippians 4:8 (NIV)

Dear friend, I pray that you may enjoy good health and that all may go well with you, even as your soul is getting along well.

3 John 1:2 (NIV)

Questions

Q: What is your mind meditating on?

List the areas where you gain your wisdom, your knowledge and your information from. Consider if it is fruitful or unfruitful.

....
....
....
....
....
....
....
....
....
....
....
....
....
....
....
....
....

Looking at your list, write each thing you have identified in the appropriate column.

Fruitful: It's producing a positive outlook on life and is God centred.

Unfruitful: It's depleting me, leaving me with a heavy heart and feeling discouraged. It's taking my eyes off God being at the centre of my life.

FRUITFUL	UNFRUITFUL

Q: For the areas you have discovered that are unfruitful, how will you make adjustments to create healthier habits?

For example, challenge yourself to go for a walk, rather than sit and look at more negative social media.

……………………………………………………………………………………………
……………………………………………………………………………………………
……………………………………………………………………………………………
……………………………………………………………………………………………
……………………………………………………………………………………………
……………………………………………………………………………………………
……………………………………………………………………………………………
……………………………………………………………………………………………
……………………………………………………………………………………………
……………………………………………………………………………………………
……………………………………………………………………………………………
……………………………………………………………………………………………
……………………………………………………………………………………………
……………………………………………………………………………………………
……………………………………………………………………………………………
……………………………………………………………………………………………
……………………………………………………………………………………………
……………………………………………………………………………………………

Day 17

TOOL NUMBER THREE: Spirit

Your spirit is your belief system which drives you on your chosen path. What you put into your mind (soul) flows into your spirit which forms all that you believe about yourself and the world around you.

Many elements of your life form the worldview that you have, including your culture, where you grew up, family and the influences you have had in your life, both beneficial and adverse.

Your spirit is central to who you are. It is where you gain your sense of purpose and it's where your hope lies. Therefore, it must be guarded and checked on regularly.

Your identity — who you are — will shape your actions. To have a true and honest view of yourself, you need to gain that truth from the One who created you — God Himself — and what He says about you.

You are accepted	1 Peter 2:9
You are redeemed	Ephesians 1:7
You are loved	Ephesians 3:18-19
You are worthy	Matthew 6:26
You are chosen	John 15:16
You are called	Galatians 1:15-16
You are a child of God	1 John 3:1
You are enough	2 Corinthians 3:5

I could unpack each and every one of these powerful God statements that He says about us, His children, but let me briefly unpack one here.

You are accepted.

At the core of our belief system is the desire to belong and be accepted. We've been created for connection and relationship. When God looks at His children, He looks at us with affirmation and approval.

Know that God created you on purpose for a purpose and He thinks highly of you.

What does the Word of God say?

Then God said, "Let Us (Father, Son, Holy Spirit) make man in Our image, according to Our likeness [not physical, but a spiritual personality and moral likeness]; and let them have complete authority over the fish of the sea, the birds of the air, the cattle, and over the entire earth, and over everything that creeps and crawls on the earth." So God created man in His own image, in the image and likeness of God He created him; male and female He created them.

Genesis 1:26-27 (NIV)

Before I formed you in the womb I knew you, before you were born, I set you apart; I appointed you as a prophet to the nations.

Jeremiah 1:5 (NIV)

But you are not like that, for you are a chosen people. You are royal priests, a holy nation, God's very own possession. As a result, you can show others the goodness of God, for He called you out of the darkness into his wonderful light.

1 Peter 2:9 (NLT)

**What infiltrates our spirit is central
to how we live our lives and what we believe.**

Q: What are some beneficial key values you live by?

....
....
....
....
....
....
....
....
....
....
....
....
....
....
....

**Remember what infiltrates our spirit
is central to how we live our lives and what we believe.**

Q: What are some damaging beliefs you have had about yourself and others?

……………………………………………………………………………………
……………………………………………………………………………………
……………………………………………………………………………………
……………………………………………………………………………………
……………………………………………………………………………………
……………………………………………………………………………………
……………………………………………………………………………………
……………………………………………………………………………………
……………………………………………………………………………………
……………………………………………………………………………………

Q: What areas of your life — be it culture, family, environment, life experiences, or something else — have helped form your personal worldview?

……………………………………………………………………………………
……………………………………………………………………………………
……………………………………………………………………………………
……………………………………………………………………………………
……………………………………………………………………………………

Q: Which are beneficial and which are damaging?

BENEFICIAL (profitable)	**DAMAGING** (unprofitable)

You've identified areas in your life that have been both beneficial (profitable) and damaging (unprofitable).

Q: Firstly, how will you protect that which is producing fruit — what is beneficial?

....
....
....
....
....
....
....

Q: Secondly, how will you bring a healthy resolve to the areas that are not producing fruit — what is damaging?

For example, you may decide to no longer allow others — or yourself — to speak wrong beliefs over you, but rather choose to soak in God's Word and believe what He says about you, and the plans and purpses He has for your life.

....
....
....
....
....
....
....
....
....
....
....
....
....
....
....
....
....
....
....

Day 18

TOOL NUMBER FOUR: Guardrails

What are guardrails?

Guardrails are simply personal boundaries /rules which you create for yourself to maintain a well-balanced life. These personal guardrails / boundaries help you measure who or what you will and will not allow into your life.

I like the analogy of a guardrail because it is a rail at the edge of something, for example, a cliff or on the deck of a boat that prevents people from falling off the edge.

If you are going to 'Step Out' into your call, you need to set goals. However, if you don't also set some guardrails in place around yourself to achieve those goals, people and things can dismantle what you set out to accomplish.

For myself, when writing my first book, I needed to put very specific guardrails around myself knowing that I could easily be distracted by other things that take my attention and stop me from fulfilling this goal. For example, I told my close friends and family who believed in my venture, to keep me accountable. They would ask me how my book was going, and tell me not to give up. I also had to be disciplined in planning out my week, otherwise I would not consider the writing of my book to be as important as other areas in my life.

Another guardrail I put in place for myself is in the area of time out. I'm one to do several things at the one time and I put 110 percent into everything I do. In the past I would just keep going, but inevitably pay the price for it, not just in my body, but emotionally also. These days, I'm more aware of what my limits are, so instead of pushing through and becoming more exhausted, I allow myself time to rest.

What does the Word of God say?

And when you find a friend, don't outwear your welcome; show up at all hours as he'll soon get fed up.

Proverbs 25:17 (MSG)

Wise people see trouble coming and get out of its way, but fools go straight to it and suffer for it.

Proverbs 22:3 (ERV)

Let your conversation be always full of grace, seasoned with salt, so that you may know how to answer everyone.

Colossians 4:6 (NIV)

Promise me, O women of Jerusalem, not to awaken love until the time is right.

Song of Solomon 8:4 (NLT)

Questions

Consider some of the guardrail necessities I have outlined below.

Score yourself from 1–5 using this scale.

1. **Great guardrail** — I believe I am balanced in this area.
2. **Good guardrail** — There is room for improvement.
3. **Ok guardrail** — I'm aware that I'm not consistent in this area.
4. **Poor guardrail** — I know I need to work on this area.
5. **No guardrail** — I didn't realise I needed a guardrail / boundary.

Time   1   2   3   4   5

I have created good time-based guardrails for non-essential activities, including socialising to make room for my personal growth.

Planning   1   2   3   4   5

I am disciplined in planning each step towards my goal — charting out my journey.

Relationships   1   2   3   4   5

I have guardrails with people — with those who will encourage and build me up as I step out, and those who will not.

Conversation   1   2   3   4   5

I have put conversation guardrails in place for myself — what I speak, listen to, or believe. I consider whether they build faith or fear in my 'step out' journey.

Spiritual   1   2   3   4   5

I am intentional with guardrails around my time with God. I am aware of distractions that keep me from spending time with Him.

Q: From this exercise what areas have you identified you need help with?

    For example, seeking support from a mentor.

....
....
....
....
....
....
....
....
....

Day 19

TOOL NUMBER FIVE: Encouragement

For a sportsperson there's nothing more encouraging than being cheered on from the grandstand; knowing those shouts of praise are just for them. It causes the player to stand tall and smile from ear to ear, because they know these shouts mean; 'We love you, we believe in you and we are barracking for you.' This is the drive that keeps a player going and causes them to push through to the end, believing they can win.

You need a cheer squad. It's very easy to get disheartened on the pathway towards your goal and your destiny. Those negative thoughts or feelings will either come from personal self-doubt or from others who will tell you it can't be done, so why bother at all? If you know you've received a God-confirming word for your call, and it's endorsed by your multitude of counsellors, then you have to stay true to that call. In doing that, you need to get around the right people — ones who will champion you. They will be your fan club. You need people around you who will say; 'You can do this. You know you are called. Just take one step at a time. You may feel like a failure today, but get up and try again tomorrow. We believe in you.'

When I wrote my first book, I knew I would need encouragers to walk alongside me. God had spoken very clearly to me to write, but my response to Him was full of self-doubt. 'God, there are so many good books out there, so many talented writers,' I said. 'Who am I to write a book?' God said, 'They don't know your story and your story is going to touch lives. The Holy Spirit will be your helper.'

To birth this book, I needed the right kind of people in my life. Ones who would not only cheer me on but also make me accountable to that call. People who would check in on me, but also be my voice of reason when I wanted to give up.

I needed this trusted group of encouragers to say to me, 'Hey Deb, how's that book going? You know you're meant to write it. You can do this Deb, don't stop writing. If God has told you to do it, He has equipped you to do it.' I also needed the help and encouragement of the Holy Spirit who would give me the anointed words to pour out onto the pages of that book, one page at a time.

Encouragement is a great gift we can give each other — it actually infuses courage into us. This tool builds strength and motivation in us to look ahead, move forward, and reach for the goal set before us. Encouragement touches the senses of our emotions which can transform our negative thoughts to a more positive outlook.

What does the Word of God say?

Since we have such a huge crowd of men of faith watching us from the grandstands, let us strip off anything that slows us down or holds us back.

Hebrews 12:1 (TLB)

And let us consider [thoughtfully] how we may encourage one another to love and to do good deeds, not forsaking our meeting together [as believers for worship and instruction], as is the habit of some, but encouraging one another; and all the more [faithfully] as you see the day [of Christ's return] approaching.

Hebrews 10:24–25 (AMP)

Questions

Identify your fan club.

These are the people who will cheer you on every step of the way. They will also be your voice of reason when you either feel like giving up or even go off track.

List those people here.

....

....

....

....

Identify your dream stealers.

Q: Who or what can steal your enthusiasm and encouragement to continue going forward?

Write them down here.

**Keep an eye on this area of your life.
The enemy for one, does not want you to succeed.**

....

....

....

....

Plan a course of action to build your fan club.

Consider who has been an encourager, a visionary or loyal friend. Invite them to be part of your 'team' to help you stay on course.

……………………………………………………………………………………
……………………………………………………………………………………
……………………………………………………………………………………
……………………………………………………………………………………
……………………………………………………………………………………
……………………………………………………………………………………
……………………………………………………………………………………
……………………………………………………………………………………
……………………………………………………………………………………
……………………………………………………………………………………
……………………………………………………………………………………
……………………………………………………………………………………
……………………………………………………………………………………
……………………………………………………………………………………
……………………………………………………………………………………
……………………………………………………………………………………
……………………………………………………………………………………
……………………………………………………………………………………
……………………………………………………………………………………
……………………………………………………………………………………

Day 20

TOOL NUMBER SIX : The Word of God

You may be thinking, 'Of course I will take my Bible. I always have my Bible with me. In fact, it's already part of my toolkit.'

It's one thing to take your Bible with you wherever you go, however it's another thing to see it as a vital part of your daily meal to feed your body, soul and spirit.

Just owning a literal Bible — the black and white, printed and bound in a nice cover Bible, is not going to do anything for you. Even your iPad, iPhone or whatever other device holds your soft copy of the Bible on screen, is not going to impact you, unless you have a heart connection with what is written within those pages. It's important when reading the Word of God, that you make time to allow what you read to sink into your belief system — your spirit. Understand that it is the God of the Bible who you're seeking and who you want to connect heart to heart with.

The word of God is alive and active, sharper than any double-edged sword. It cuts all the way through, to where soul and spirit meet, to where joints and marrow come together. It judges the desires and thoughts of the heart. Hebrews 4:12 (GNT)

The Word is living.
Think about that for a moment. This indicates that the Word has breath. If you understand this truth, you will know that the God breathed word into your heart, is life-giving. It has transforming power to change you, grow you, strengthen you and deliver you.

The Word is active.
The God of the Bible is active. Active speaks of energy, functioning, moving, creating, engaging and of being effective. God will actively do what He says He will do.

The Word is sharper than any double-edged sword.
A physical sword can pierce the body. People see the effects of where that sword has entered. The spiritual sword of God, pierces the heart — it not only convicts us of sin, but also resonates deep within our spirit where life changes happen. People see the effects of the spiritual sword.

Think of the Word of God as a 'must have' vitamin which feeds your immune system. Your body's immune system will falter if you don't have the right vitamins feeding it. It's the same with feeding on the Word of God. You'll falter if you aren't immersing yourself in the living, active God-breathed vitamins of heaven.

What does the Word of God say?

This book of instruction must not depart from your mouth; you are to meditate on it day and night so that you may carefully observe everything written in it. For then you will prosper and succeed in whatever you do.

Joshua 1:8 (CSB)

All Scripture is God-breathed [given by divine inspiration] and is profitable for instruction, for conviction [of sin], for correction [of error and restoration to obedience], for training in righteousness [learning to live in conformity to God's will, both publicly and privately — behaving honourably with personal integrity and moral courage]; so that the man of God may be complete and proficient, outfitted and thoroughly equipped for every good work.

2 Timothy 3:16-17 (AMP)

Consequently, faith comes from hearing the message, and the message is heard through the Word about Christ.

Romans 10:17 (NIV)

Questions

Q: How often are you partaking of your spiritual 'vitamins'? Be honest.

....

Q: What are some ways you can ensure you get your regular dose?

> For example, use a ready-made devotional. There are many available online. The YouVersion app has great devotionals with a variety of topics to choose from.

....
....
....
....

Q: What are some ways you can plan your time in order to soak in the Word of God?

Remember what soaks into your spirit is what you live out of.

....
....
....
....
....
....

Day 21

TOOL NUMBER SEVEN: The Holy Spirit

Together with the Word of God, we must carry with us the Holy Spirit. We cannot travel this road without Him.

Who is the Holy Spirit? He is the third person of the Godhead; Father, Son and Holy Spirit. He is not number three, but one of three — all of who is one God.

Prior to Jesus ascending into Heaven, He told His disciples that He must leave in order for the comforter, the Holy Spirit, to come. Why? Because it would be the Holy Spirit living in us and working through us to take the Gospel into nations across the earth, from generation to generation.

The Holy Spirit is our guide, our comforter and our encourager. He is patient and kind. He will wait with us for as long as it takes, but at the same time gently nudging us along, each stage of our journey.

The Holy Spirit is our teacher and our wise counsellor. He intercedes for us when we have no adequate words to speak. He empowers us to do the work of the ministry, He appoints gifts to us for the work of the ministry, and He sheds light on His Holy Word in order for us to understand it's spiritual meaning and practical application for our lives.

He anoints us with power to speak boldly when necessary and whisper where required, and He loves to speak words of encouragement to us and assure us that we are His.

He will walk beside us every step of the way, and when we are still and tune our ears into His whisper, we will hear Him say, 'Keep going, you can do this.'

What does the Word of God say?

When they finished praying, the place where they were meeting was shaken. They were all filled with the Holy Spirit and began to proclaim God's message with boldness.

Acts 4:31 (GNT)

Those who are led by God's Spirit are God's children. For the Spirit that God has given you does not make you slaves and cause you to be afraid; instead, the Spirit makes you God's children, and by the Spirit's power we cry out to God, "Father! My Father!" God's Spirit joins himself to our spirits to declare that we are God's children.

Romans 8:14-16 (GNT)

We must thank God at all times for you, friends, you whom the Lord loves. For God chose you as the first to be saved by the Spirit's power to make you His holy people and by your faith in the truth.

2 Thessalonians 2:13 (GNT)

And you also became God's people when you heard the true message, the Good News that brought you salvation. You believed in Christ, and God put His stamp of ownership on you by giving you the Holy Spirit He had promised.

Ephesians 1:13 (GNT)

The Spirit's presence is shown in some way in each person for the good of all. The Spirit gives one person a message full of wisdom, while to another person the same Spirit gives a message full of knowledge. One and the same Spirit gives faith to one person, while to another person He gives the power to heal. The Spirit gives one person the power to work miracles; to another, the gift of speaking God's message; and to yet another, the ability to tell the difference between gifts that come from the Spirit and those that do not. To one person He gives the ability to speak in strange tongues, and to another He gives the ability to explain what is said. But it is one and the same Spirit who does all this; as He wishes, He gives a different gift to each person.

1 Corinthians 12:7-11 (GNT)

When, however, the Spirit comes, who reveals the truth about God, He will lead you into all the truth. He will not speak on His own authority, but He will speak of what He hears and will tell you of things to come. He will give me glory, because He will take what I say and tell it to you. All that my Father has is mine; that is why I said that the Spirit will take what I give Him and tell it to you.

John 16:13-15 (GNT)

But when the Holy Spirit comes upon you, you will be filled with power, and you will be witnesses for me in Jerusalem, in all of Judea and Samaria, and to the ends of the earth.

Acts 1:8 (GNT)

Questions

Q: How acquainted are you with the Holy Spirit?

Take a moment to read the scriptures in the section 'What does the Word of God say?' again.

Write down what God's speaking to you about in these verses regarding the Holy Spirit.

....
....
....
....
....
....
....
....
....
....
....
....
....
....
....
....

Reflection Time

LET'S TAKE A MOMENT TO REFLECT ON HOW FAR YOU HAVE COME

First of all, congratulations. You've made it all the way through this devotional.

Score Yourself.

If you were to give yourself a score out of 10 (10 being the best scenario), where are you sitting at this point?

1. I know I have some work to do.
5. I'm getting there.
10. I'm right where I need to be.

BODY - I'm working on having a healthier lifestyle.

1   2   3   4   5   6   7   8   9   10

SOUL - I've exchanged unfruitful environments/social media/other, for fruitful ones.

1   2   3   4   5   6   7   8   9   10

SPIRIT - I'm believing what God says about me, rather than the negative influence.

1   2   3   4   5   6   7   8   9   10

GUARDRAILS - I've created some necessary guardrails for myself.

1   2   3   4   5   6   7   8   9   10

ENCOURAGEMENT - I'm establishing my encouragement team.

1   2   3   4   5   6   7   8   9   10

THE WORD OF GOD - I've put a plan in place to spend time in God's Word.

1   2   3   4   5   6   7   8   9   10

THE HOLY SPIRIT - I'm meditating on the Word to hear the Holy Spirit speaking.

1   2   3   4   5   6   7   8   9   10

For the areas you are moving forward in, give yourself a high five and celebrate. For the areas you need to adjust, don't beat yourself up, but instead, congratulate yourself for being honest in identifying them.

Remember, working on life disciplines take time.

Congratulations

You made it to the end of this 21-day devotional. Yay! You are serious about pursuing the call of God on your life. I hope you have already begun to 'Step Out'. You will not regret it.

This 21-day devotional has been written as a roadmap to help you navigate your journey and see you continue to move forward. Keep making the necessary adjustments, and although you have finished this 21-day devotional, use it as your guide moving forward.

Tips to keep you motivated

- Continue to re-examine the areas you need to strengthen and grow in.
- Reassess your answers to the questions to see if they have changed.
- Keep focused on your own journey.
- Don't compare your journey to other's journey.
- Journal your journey.
- Establish your cheer squad. Mentors, encouragers and/or coaches.
- Check your toolkit. Do you have your seven tools for the journey intact?
- Trust God in your journey.

Don't be one who at the end of your life says; 'I wish I had.' Be one who says; 'I'm glad I did.'

Deborah Hilton

Stay connected

You can contact me via the links below.

Email: deborahhilton101@gmail.com

Blogspace: debsblog.space/

Facebook: facebook.com/IsayYES

Appendix

ucl.ac.uk/news/2009/aug/how-long-does-it-take-form-habit

https://www.azquotes.com/quotes/topics/mustard-seed.html

https://pastors.com/7-benefits-of-praising-god/

Books by Deborah Hilton

Just Say YES - You can trust God in your journey.

What is the difference between those who do and those who don't? What is the mark of those living out their purpose and those who aren't? The difference is right in front of you. It's you. It starts with you. Every successful person begins with those two ingredients, choosing, and moving. So, are you ready? The first step is always the hardest, so if you have chosen to do that, well done!

Available as a paperback or e-book at all online book stores including; Apple Books, Amazon, Kobo and Ebay.

Out of Control - God can do more with our relinquished control than we can do by holding onto it.

What do you associate with this statement, 'Out Of Control'? I am sure you have heard people say, 'She is completely out of control,' or 'He has totally lost it!' This is usually what we think of when that statement is voiced. However, the 'out of control' I am talking about is when, at times, you find yourself dropping the proverbial juggling balls in the life that you believe you were meant to be in control of.

Whatever we personally brand control as, to some degree, we all want it. We want to know that everything is safe and secure in our world, which is both a normal and natural expectation for our life.

Available as a paperback or e-book at all online book stores including; Koorong, Apple Books, Amazon, Kobo and Ebay.

www.ingramcontent.com/pod-product-compliance
Lightning Source LLC
Chambersburg PA
CBHW070612010526
44118CB00012B/1495